YOUR KNOWLEDGE HAS VALUE

Alex Ngumbi

Talbots Clothing Company: Market Entry Plan in Chinese Market

GRIN Verlag

Bibliografische Information der Deutschen Nationalbibliothek:

Die Deutsche Bibliothek verzeichnet diese Publikation in der Deutschen National-
bibliografie; detaillierte bibliografische Daten sind im Internet über http://dnb.d-
nb.de/ abrufbar.

Imprint:

Copyright © 2012 GRIN Verlag GmbH
Druck und Bindung: Books on Demand GmbH, Norderstedt Germany
ISBN: 978-3-656-55479-0

This book at GRIN:

http://www.grin.com/en/e-book/265540/talbots-clothing-company-market-entry-
plan-in-chinese-market

GRIN - Your knowledge has value

Der GRIN Verlag publiziert seit 1998 wissenschaftliche Arbeiten von Studenten, Hochschullehrern und anderen Akademikern als eBook und gedrucktes Buch. Die Verlagswebsite www.grin.com ist die ideale Plattform zur Veröffentlichung von Hausarbeiten, Abschlussarbeiten, wissenschaftlichen Aufsätzen, Dissertationen und Fachbüchern.

Visit us on the internet:

http://www.grin.com/

http://www.facebook.com/grincom

http://www.twitter.com/grin_com

Talbots Clothing Company –

Market Entry Plan in Chinese Market

Table of Contents

1. Introduction..2

2. PART A Company & Industry Analysis...2

    2.1. Company Overview 2

    2.2. Chinese Clothing Industry 2

3. PART B Selection of Key Markets and Analysis 3

    3.1. SWOT ANALYSIS...4

4. PART C- In Depth Market Analysis of Target EE Market...6

    4.1. PESTLE ANALYSIS..6

5. PART D Entry Strategy Plan 9

6. Recommendations..10

7. Conclusions..11

References..12

1. Introduction

The main aim of this report is to propose a market entry strategy for an organization in an emerging economic market. The paper has chosen Talbots Womenwear company to expand in emerging economic market namely China market. The paper uses PESTEL method to examine the market and analyzes the current market situation using SWOT model and proposes a market entry strategy for the company.

2. PART A Company & Industry Analysis

2.1. Company Overview

The Talbots is an area of expertise in retailing and direct marketer of classic clothing of women's accessories and shoes. The firm mainly functions in Canada and the United States. It's headquarter is located in Hingham, Massachusetts and nearly 9,096 employees work in this company, whereas 5,612 work as part-timers. This firm recorded earnings of $1,213.1 million during the fiscal year which completed in January 2011, which was considered a reduction of 1.8% in comparison to FY 2010. The functioning income of the firm was $31.4 million in FY 2011, in comparison to a functioning loss of nearly $8.7 million in FY 2010. Hence, the net income was estimated as $10.8 million in FY 2011, in comparison with the total loss of $29.4 million in FY 2010 (Talbots, 2013).

The Talbots is an area of expertise in retailing and direct marketer of classic clothing of women's accessories and shoes. The firm got into a contract with Li & Fung in the year 2009 in August and from that time Li & Fung has been the worldwide clothing sourcing agent of the company for most of its clothing. This assists the company in improving the geographic dispersal of its goods sourcing; decrease functional costs and increase its functional effectiveness. Nevertheless, low customer confidence and high rate of unemployment could unfavorably affect the requirement for the products of the Talbots (Anderson, 2010).

2.2. Chinese Clothing Industry

With the fast progress in current years, it has made China capable to have the biggest clothing industry across the globe. It is mostly because of the truth that China possesses a large and low-priced labor force as well as raw materials' sufficient supply. Hence, the apparel is China's one of the leader industries. China is the foremost exporter particularly in the field of fashion and plays a vital role in the economy of global textile. The causes for China to be the foremost exporter in the area of trend are because of massive inflows of foreign investment, low labor cost etc. European Union used to restrict business with China by putting protectionist policies; however the Multi Fiber Agreement ended in the year 2005 (Bradley, 2008).

The increment of new budding apparel exporting nations and the rise in costs of labor in the costal areas because of the enhanced living standards are risks to the apparel industry China. These modifications caused the clothing industry to get into in an intermediary phase in structural and geographical factors as well as institutional factors. The production in China is conquered by huge production of fundamental products, yet with altering customers' demands this industry has had to slowly begin new technologies for manufacturing, designing and merchandising.. Wang, who is Chinese Textile Company's marketing director states that it's very easy for foreign firms to find and set up a relationship with subcontractors of China, because Chinese firm would like to draw foreign investment and carry out internationally. The companies of China are also competent to provide foreign investors what they have been searching for. It's helpful to foreign investors as well as Chinese manufactures (Phizacklea, 2000).

3. PART B Selection of Key Markets and Analysis

The apparel and non-apparel of China and production market has faced strong, although decelerating, development from the year 2008. This market was expected to improve in the year 2012. The apparel and non-apparel of Chinese production market had complete incomes of $228.9 billion in the year 2011, which represented a compound yearly rate of growth of 12 percentages between the year 2007 and the year 2011 (Lam, 2006). In evaluation, the market of Japan declined with a CARC of -0.9 percentages, and the market of India showed growth with a CAGR of 11 percentages, over the same time, so as to reach individual values. The segment of non-apparel was the most lucrative offer of the market in the year 2011, with overall incomes of $119.6 billion, equal to 52.2 percentages of the overall value of the market. The segment of apparel contributed income of $109.3 billion in the year 2011. Somewhat, the markets of Japan will turn down with a CARC of -0.9 percentages, and the market of India will grow with a CAGR of 15 (Mayrhofer, 2004).

3.1. SWOT ANALYSIS

Strength

The Chinese clothing market provides an excellent merchandise opportunity. The merchandising policies of the company can focus on setting up superior consumer contentment and consumers' experience through its pledge to price, style and quality. Since the goods are designed and conceptualized in-house, the Talbots not just saves on expenses to produce greater gross margins, but provides merchandise in line too with the trends of the fashion. And the merchandising team of the company designs accessories and apparel for the consumers to assemble total outfits. Sales acquaintances also assist customers in selection of merchandise and coordination of wardrobe. Consequently, the merchandising strategy of the company can even assist in making better the loyalty of the customer by enhancing the shopping experience of the customer (Bradley, 2008).

Weaknesses

Lawsuit in Chinese Market in opposition to Talbots might affect income margin Talbots is engaged in a lawful proceeding on the topic of misleading and false statements offered to its investors. On February 3, in the year 2011 a complaint was lodged in the United States District Court for the District of Massachusetts in opposition to Talbots and a few of its officers. It was alleged that the firm had made some misleading and false statements and omitted a few material information that artificially raised the market price of its general stock between 8th December, 2009 and 11th January, 2011. These litigations could influence the image of the company in a negative manner and resulting harms could raise the cost of the company and force its productivity (Chandra, 2012).

Opportunities

There is an excellent growth in positive trends in e-commerce market to drive sales within Chinese Clothing Industry. The online channel has gained popularity as customers opt for the channel because of convenience and low costs. Studies show that sales of e-commerce are observing significant growth in comparison with whole retail sales in the United States. The fashion is anticipated to persist in the future.

The direct marketing section of the goods with the help of internet, catalog, and red-line channels of phone. In the FY2011, direct marketing section accounted for 18.3 percentages of the total revenues of the company. Also, the internet channel added 73 percentages of the whole direct marketing sales in the FY2010. Revenues that were made from direct marketing section of the firm raised by 6.7 percent in the FY 2011 over the FY 2010. In the year 2009, Talbots can make several changes in its website to enable it additionally user-friendly. The firm continues to make attempts to additionally refine the visual content and the functionality of its website. The focus of this company on internet section coupled with altering trends in customer's behavior of buying and the reputation of online channel could influence the revenues positively (Colton & Bearden, 2010).

The footwear market and cosmetics' market has indicated strong development in the current times in the China. According to study, the fashion footwear industry of China had touched $34,611 million in the year 2010, which represented a rise of 7.2 percent over the earlier year. The footwear's sale in the category of women had accounted for 60 percentage of the incomes of the total fashion footwear industry, which followed by the category of men which was 30% and the category of children which was 10%. On fashion footwear, spending by women rose by 8 percentages in the year 2010, whereas spending by men rose by nearly 7 percentages in the year 2010 over the earlier year. Footwear structures a vital offering at the retail outlets of the Talbots. The increasing demand for trendy footwear in the China might lead to additional consumer's traffic at the retail outlets of the company and drive incomes from the category of the products (Doole, International Marketing Strategy: Analysis, Development and Implementation, 2008).

Threats

China's labor cost is increasing drastically. Nearly 41.5 percentages of its products are obtained from China. Growing labor cost in the nation would influence the cost of the Talbots. According to the sources of the industry, Chinese minimum wages rose by about 22 percentages in the year 2011. This was due to the fact that the government had initiated to raise the income levels of the Chinese. At the end of the year 2011 (September), 21 out of 31 provinces of China raised minimum wages with an average of 21.7 percentages. A few of the provinces were anticipated to raise their minimum wage at the end of the year 2011. Additionally, compared with different emerging markets, cost of labor in China is turning to be more costly. The comparative cost of production in China would almost surely increase as the costs of labor increase. Passing on the rise in costs to consumers who are more and more becoming price alert is a competitive drawback. Following several years of profound

5

clearance acts, Talbots has been encountering problems of getting back to a normal price model. Hence, increase in labor cost of Chinese combined with low level capability to leave behind the costs to consumers could influence margins of Talbots adversely (Colton & Bearden, 2010).

4. PART C- In Depth Market Analysis of Target EE Market
4.1. PESTLE ANALYSIS

Political

In China the geopolitical influence is increasing overtime. China keeps on in forging good ties with several nations, and its sphere of impact is clearly obvious in Africa. The trade value of China with Africa increased from $40bn in the year 2005 to $127bn in the year 2010. Chinese growing influence in Africa has not merely been restricted to trade, nevertheless, as it has provided the nation entry to oil reserves too. Furthermore, China had put money around 20% of its entire external investment between the year 2005 and the year 2010 in Africa. Also, its investment might rise by 70 percentages to $50bn by the year 2015. It has driven to a huge rise in the impact of China in Africa. Also, the CPC experiences from factional competition that are increasing to the lead of the CPC congress (Mueller, 1989).

The changing political situation within Chinese market is highly likely to hit the growth of various industries among which Chinese Clothing industry too is one and the foreign companies like Talbots might get impacted due to this.

Economic

Chinese GDP growth is averaged nearly 12.55 percentages during the period of the year 2004 and 2011, which was considerably more than the rates of growth obtained during the year 1980s and the year 1990s. Actual GDP growth decreased from 10.3 percentages in the year 2010 to 9.1 percentages in the year 2011 in consequence of decreasing exports and crisis of the lingering euro zone. The irregular development in China in regards to the town and the country is also a matter of concern. There has been a large gap with regards to economic development, income and living standards among the urban influential people and the poor people rural area. As indicated by official data, revenues in country areas are almost 1/3 of those in metropolitan areas (Burt, 2000).

Southeast and East China are developed much more than the poor West and North China. The extremely industrialized east coast of the country represents a bleak difference with the poor neighborhood of the areas dotted with racial minorities and western provinces. Uneven growth is the main challenge of the nation in the medium term (Onkvisit & Shaw, 2008).

The EU (European Union) and the United States describe for the major parts of the exports of China. Hence, China remains susceptible to external requirement from the European Union and the United States. In case there is full-blown problem in the European Union, then the huge exporters of China might be hit. It could rise unemployment and drive to plunging housing prices. Furthermore, the contagion risks of the economy are greater, like a full-blown debt crisis of European would drive to a problem of capital flows that could in return drive to low inflows of FDI. Additionally, this might hurt foreign ventures that the economy of China depends upon. Eventually, the debt crisis of European might become a grave threat to the economy of China.

Therefore, it is very important that Talbots ventures in this emerging economy cautiously focusing on all the economic threats discussed above.

Social

One of the Chinese longstanding crises has been its growing population. Its implementation of the one-child strategy has shown result in the rate of population growth decreasing drastically; however, conversely it has enabled China a nation with a more and more aging population. This is because of the fact that the progress in life expectancy has taken place over the years. Even though there had been a common decline in the levels of poverty, services of healthcare are mainly based in towns, enabling them unreachable to those who live in backward areas In spite of its successes, the policy of one-child implemented in China is generating a rising number of crisis too (Hines & Bruce, 2012).

The population that is aging will put pressure on healthcare and social safety. It is guessed that by the year 2050 1/3 of the entire population of China would be more than 60 years. According to the study of a government committee, nearly 10 million careers were in demand whilst merely 100,000 were offered in the year 2011. Care facilities of China fulfill demand for just 1.6 percentages of people more than 60 years old. Citizens, who were above 65, constituted nearly 8.85 percentages of the population of China, in the year 2011. It had been projected that it might grow to nearly 12 percentages by the year 2020. There would be 2 working age citizens supporting one individual more than 60 years by the year 2030, an increase from 6 working people who supported 1 person above 60 in the year 2000. This growth in the aging population might lead to a decrease in productive yield in the coming years, which might be a grave problem provided that the economy of China greatly depends on a large team of young workers getting low wages. China might lose its price competiveness and its development story might come to a crushing halt if the fast demographic modification is not captured in time (Hines & Bruce, 2012).

All in all, Chinese population is increasing rapidly and so does the demand for the clothing products. Therefore, Talbots can utilize this opportunity efficiently.

Technological

Over the years, several Chinese political leaders of China, which includes the present president, were/are from technological backgrounds. It has resulted in positive policies from the political category toward the development of technology. China too has a big number of R&D organizations, which means the nation is well-equipped for modern research. Nevertheless, money is spent on furthering the agenda of party more willingly than stimulating research of main concern. In addition, examiners are given very less money in China in comparison to other nations, which means that there is very little incentive for a potential candidate to get into the area of research. It has influenced the number of quality consumers who follow this way (Phizacklea, 2000).

The number of online users for online shopping is also increasing rapidly in this market. The Talbots can make use of this opportunity by enhancing its online sales portal.

Legal

Decentralized court system of China permits the judiciary to fix several issues at the level of the grassroots. There are several other lawful bodies too that fix various disputes. Lawful processes to open up trade have declined over a period of time, which results in extra FDI flowing into the nation. Nevertheless, there would be future threats as a result of feeble corporate laws as well as be short of resources at the level of the judicial. Political interference in lawful matters is one more detrimental cause. China has been utilizing stringent steps against them who are spotted criticizing the government. People criticizing state bodies are at threat of getting severe punishment. They would even be blamed of false allegations like "inciting subversion." There has been increased repression of crowd collection by the police in metros, citing factors of stability preservation. There has forever been serious censorship of the internet and the media, particularly social media (Anderson, 2010).

Environmental

China has in nature diverse atmosphere, with vast fields of land under covered under forest. Even though the nation has a comprehensive ecological framework, the accomplishment of these strategies is not very effectual. Pollution in all its types has reached highest levels, with China lately overtaking the United States in terms of consumption of fuel (Wind, 1986).

5. PART D Entry Strategy Plan

As per the findings from the analysis conducted, it is recommended that Talbots enforces franchising as the market entry strategy to venture in Chinese market.

The system of franchising could be stated as a type of system in which owners (franchisees) of semi-independent trade pay royalties and fees to a main company (franchiser) in turn for the ownership to get recognized with its trademark, so as to sell its services or products, and over and over again to utilize its trade system and format. In comparison to licensing, franchising contracts inclines to be longer as well as the franchisor provides a broader package of authorities and resources. Additionally, whilst a licensing agreement includes things like trade secrets, intellectual property, and others whilst in franchising it's restricted to trademarks (Mueller, 1989).

The chief success for doing franchise is to avert sharing the strategic act with any franchisee particularly if that act is considered significant to the firm. Sharing those policies act may raise the franchisee's potential to be our future opponent because of the knowledge.

6. Recommendations

It's an imperative affair to examine rationally clothing industry of China's competitive benefits in the reengineering of worldwide textile distribution chain. Taking into account the favorable and unfavorable causes confronted by apparel industry at the after-quota age, there are several countermeasures for it which are given below (Lam, 2006).

In order to create a deep foothold in the emerging economy of China, it is recommended that Talbot utilizes the below steps as its marketing strategies.

Brand development

Brand rivalry has already turned to be a main part of market rivalry. It doesn't just mean to enhance the famousness of name. Organizations should bestow their brands with great cultural meanings and grow multiple brand policies. Like clothing designers are involved in their designs, the necessary idea is to provide prominence to characteristics of domestic culture and culture of the nation.

Merely by making best utilization of the carrier, mainly the apparel, and showing Chinese culture, we could set up the place of "Chinese clothing". In the procedure of supporting some of head firms to form various industrial clusters, we need to focus on the compliance of brands and resources (Mayrhofer, 2004).

Total costs superiority strategy

In the macro feature, clothing industry of China possesses a unique place in global clothing business. It possesses a bright prospect in the area of export. Nevertheless, China clothing's aggressive advantage mainly concentrates on the price feature. It doesn't have a major benefit concerning with the costs of the production. Hence, Chinese firms need to make up policies as a whole and select the functional mode that could help in realizing maximum incomes at lowest costs. Thus, the clothing industry of China would be strong. Talbot must attempt to gain necessary advantages in labors prices, materials costs etc (Talbots, 2013).

Technique talent and Standard qualification strategy

For any new firm, skill is one of main competences. Innovation in the field of technology is the root for firms to enhance their competence. Firms have a rising demand for skills. They put emphasis on the cultivation and exploration of talents.

In current years attestation has turned to be one of needs listed in multi-national orders of the firms increasingly. It has by now served as a technology hurdle for the export of China. It is a type of adjustment of rivalry between developing nations and developed nations in the global market. Taking into account this trend, clothing enterprises of China and Chinese government need to take action (Onkvisit & Shaw, 2008).

Supply chain advantage strategy

Supply chain management has by now gained increasingly attentions from firms. It has slowly become a choice for the growth policy of modern firms. On the contrary with the traditional vertical management method, the supply chain management possesses enormous competitive benefits. The supply chain management could offer with not just a system but an organizational form too in resource distribution (Phizacklea, 2000).

7. Conclusions

All in all, as per the study conducted the Chinese market features a high rate of growth opportunity for clothing industry. It is recommended that Talbots implements the franchising strategy to venture in this international market and also uses the recommended strategy above to prosper further in this emerging economy.

References

Anderson, E. (2010). International Market Entry and Expansion via Independent or Integrated Channels of Distribution. *Journal of Marketing;* , 23-69.

Bradley, F. (2008). *International Marketing strategy* (Vol. II). London: Gomin publishers.

Burt, S. (2000). The role of store image in retail internationalisation. . *International Marketing Review*, p433.

Cavusgil, S. (2012). Reflections on international marketing: destructive regeneration and multinational firms. *Journal of the Academy of Marketing Science, 14*, 45-89.

Chan, P. Y. (2010). FASHION RETAILING IN CHINA: AN EXAMINATION OF ITS DEVELOPMENT AND ISSUES. . *Advances in International Marketing;*, 75-110.

Chandra, Y. (2012). An Opportunity-Based View of Rapid Internationalization. *Journal of International Marketing;, 20*(1), 74-102.

Colton, D. A., & Bearden, W. O. (2010). Drivers of International E-Tail Performance: The Complexities of Orientations and Resources. *Journal of International Marketing;, 18*(1), 1-22.

Czinkota, M. R. (2007). *International Marketing.* London: Cengage Learning.

Doole, I. (2008). *International Marketing Strategy: Analysis, Development and Implementation.* London: springer.

Doole, I., & Lowe, R. (2008). *International marketing strategy: analysis, development and implementation.* Cengage Learning EMEA,.

Hines, T., & Bruce, M. (2012). *Fashion Marketing: Contemporary Issues.* london: sage.

Isobel Doole, R. L. (2008). *International marketing strategy: analysis, development and implementation.* New York: Cengage Learning EMEA.

Lam, J. K. (2006). Textile and apparel supply chain management in Hong Kong. *International Journal of Clothing Science & Technology*, 265-277.

Mayrhofer, U. (2004). International Market Entry: Does the Home Country Affect Entry-Mode Decisions? *Journal of International Marketing;*, 12-96.

Mueller, B. (1989). Multinational advertising: factors influencing the standardised vs. specialised approach. *International Marketing Review*, 7-18.

Onkvisit, S., & Shaw, J. J. (2008). *International marketing: strategy and theory* (Vol. 12). London: Taylor & Francis.

Phizacklea, A. (2000). *Unpacking the Fashion Industry.* London: SAGE.

Talbots. (2013). The Talbots, Inc., SWOT ANALYSIS. . *Talbots, Inc. SWOT Analysis;*, 11.

Wind, Y. (1986). Guidelines for Developing International Marketing Strategies. *Journal of Marketing;*, 23.